The Starlight Room

poems by

Lesley Valdes

Finishing Line Press
Georgetown, Kentucky

The Starlight Room

Copyright © 2025 by Lesley Valdes
ISBN 979-8-89990-109-6 First Edition
All rights reserved under International and Pan-American Copyright Conventions. No part of this book may be reproduced in any manner whatsoever without written permission from the publisher, except in the case of brief quotations embodied in critical articles and reviews.

Many thanks to the editors of the following journals in which these poems first appeared, some in earlier versions:

Shadowgraph	Clewiston
The Boiler	At the corner store
Philadelphia Poets	The pianist speaks, Found
Moonstone Anthology	Thief
Muse House Journal	When Philip Wu took us to the Chinese banquet
The Curator	Miami
The Innisfree Poetry Journal	At the tag sale, a chair
Glint Literary Journal	Attend
Schuylkill Valley Journal	At the good dog park
Women's Voices for Change	At the corner store
Pantheon Magazine	The Starlight Room

Publisher: Leah Huete de Maines
Editor: Christen Kincaid
Cover Art: Jennifer Macdonald
Author Photo: Johana Macdonald
Cover Design: Elizabeth Maines McCleavy

Order online: www.finishinglinepress.com
also available on amazon.com

Author inquiries and mail orders:
Finishing Line Press
PO Box 1626
Georgetown, Kentucky 40324
USA

Contents

I. It's not about the sharps and the flats.

Clewiston 1
Listening to Art Tatum 2
Miami 3
The things she left 4
Found 5
Listening to the death of Lorca 6
The pianist speaks 8
Legato 9

II. Music depends on its own diminishing . . .

At the corner store 13
At the tag sale, a chair 14
Art 15
Thief 16
Salvage 17
At the good dog park 18
When Phillip Wu took us to the Chinese banquet, ... 19
Attend 20
Quodlibet 21

III. It is all a matter of hands.

Adagio, ma non troppo 25
Finding Schubert 26
On the ceiling in the Spanish Chapel 30
319 E. 24th St. #25D 31
Fermata 32
The Starlight Room 33
Flamboyant 35

Notes 36
Gratitude 37

For Jennifer Madeline and Johana Caroline Macdonald

Olga Llaneza Valdes

Joan Hutton Landis

who led the way

It's not about the sharps and the flats, it's about how it makes you feel.
Leonard Bernstein

Clewiston

I saw them again
I thought it was a dream.
Then I remembered
yesterday at Las Cruces
where I get the avocado and cilantro
where they never mind the dog.

Canes thick as clenched fists
leaning tall, unraveling
as if they've bundled themselves.

>   Father swerving the Chevy off the road
>   to show us how to cut
>   and where to sip. Ignoring
>   Mother's *Serge, we're trespassing!*

Sneaking through the canes
sweeter than the syrup.

Listening to Art Tatum, I think about my father

Those easy arpeggios up and down the keys
the unexpected runs and turns like Tatum

> who turned a keyboard inside out
> whose fingers danced.

My father's band at the Doral,
mother kept a scrapbook.

> The lights impersonating starlight in the Starlight Room
> eighth notes and 32nds chuckling across the stage
>
> Dad at the keys, joy spilling.

I have a postcard of Duke Ellington rushing
somewhere. The tux, the glee, that smile

> so like my father's.
> He never hurried

those feathery turns that made me want
to rush to save them.

> Pearls that split too quick their silk.

Miami

Houses painted like the inside of fruit.
Mango, guava,
papaya with beady eyes.
Houses with roofs like ski hats
low under the dome sky.

Casas with lawns like sloppy houses.
Casas gated and manicured
where egrets wander
haunted by bromeliads,
strange ferns. Casas
always with pools.
No one in them.

City of moonlight
cacophony, decay.
Roads named for conquerors
and birds.
O Miami!
Medley of voices.

Let's get a cortadito.

The things she left

Her eyes were amber
clip-ons. The kind they wore in 1963

the week the president was shot
the night I woke perspiring. Earrings

 where her eyes should be.

They sent my young aunt's silks and suits
jewelry—even the costume stuff.

She had to miss them.
Or do the things we miss, miss us?

Bracelets thick with charms
that open intricate as clockwork.

Moss silvering the oaks,
the river house.

She wasn't beautiful, Madeline
until you knew her.

They sent the china hen she filled with Hershey Kisses
for the kids she couldn't have.

All the pretty things
I'm wearing.

Found

for Sergio

To be a gardener spellbound
to stand a vigil listening to cabbages, potatoes,

the crescent moon.
Your brother is lost, she says.

The priests are gone.
Where are the trade winds?

Your brother is lost.

Lost as the bandoneon
that likes its sad and

necessary music. The sea
is lost and found and lost—

Accepting.

Time's ticking, the stranger says,
eyes watering.

Your brother is lost.

Lost as the squeezebox
of the necessary.

The priests are gone.
Time's ticking.

Where are the trade winds?

The bandoneon likes being lost.
Sad squeezebox.

And you, my brother?

Listening to the death of Lorca

>After   *Ainadamar*, 2006.
>Osvaldo Golijov, composer,
>David Henry Hwang, libretto.

At the opera, a lone soprano grieving
and sweet shock—girls chanting cante jondo.

At the opera, rifles multiplying.
A firing squad. Collage of thudding heels

Assasination by flamenco.
He didn't care much for flamenco.

The music turns to wind, to water
to make a poetry of murder. Water

gurgling from a fountain
grieving over stones.

Horses galloping on stones.

There are horses in the soul of Lorca.
I don't know where this comes from, the line is true.

Ainadamar. The fountain at Alhambra
where they think he died.

Every afternoon in Granada, a child dies.
He wrote this.

Every afternoon or morning (the hour's still unknown)
his turn.

They're singing now, the wind, the water —

At the Huntington in San Marino, trees more splendid
than the art. Ruby seeds in carmine fruit. Musica callada

the silent music.
In the garden at the Huntington

I saw the pomegranates bleeding melody.
In Spain a pomegranate is *granada*.

Lorca.

The pianist speaks

> *Most of what I know about myself, I've learned from playing Schumann.*
> Jonathan Biss

I can't explain exactly but I think I understand.
Something in the inner voices in the middle register
harmonies that reach don't overreach
the way an ordinary life is lived.

Schumann gives you human voices, my daughter said.
We heard the pianist at Marlboro with another protégé.
Biss looking inward, the other virtuoso suggesting ownership,
a touch of arrogance.

Schumann wasn't arrogant.

The falling tones that catch inside the throat.
The harmony as melody. Accompaniments so beautiful
      I play the *Dichterliebe* without a singer, Johana said.

She's leaving home, it's time.
Frauen-liebe und leben.

Legato

Touch
          as if you can't let go

The way that lovers
          hate to leave

Bend what doesn't bend
          so the tune curves

Touch, that's the thing
          a hundred ways

A hundred ways.

Music depends on its own diminishing .....

    Ellen Bryant Voight

At the corner store

Strawberries alone in an ovoid glass and each
the same squat size and shape and I thought of hearts
suspended. In the syrup you could see the pinprick pores.

He took me to fields of strawberries when I was nine. Rows of low-
blooming ovals perched under green. He must have remembered they were
my favorite that they blossomed my birthday month. I remember him in
another row

calling out to slow down (how often he told me that) leave some
for someone else. Scratch of earth, mess of knees, gobbling bounty
under the Florida sun. Mother scolding about the rash. Calamine.

A day to ourselves and nothing of what was said father-to-daughter-
to-father on the long drive home but he wasn't a talker you felt
the words. Only once in the car

When your time's up, it's up, he said. I must have asked about the war,
I was newly married then. We didn't know he was sick. How calm he was
everything deliberate, a soft adagio, except the cancer the quick year time
suspended.

At the tag sale, a chair

>After *Animus.* 5' x 4.5' x 2.5'
>patinated unique cast bronze.
>Jennifer Macdonald. 1997

Dark wood, ladder-back.
Rush seat for hips ampler
than mine.

Whose?
Looked old.

You want what?
your father said.

Just married.
We needed a bed.

But the chair—
laddering hopes
to home—to daughters
unborn.

How you scrambled
to the chair, traced the slats
smoothed the curl at the top
like a wave or Napoleon hat.

Art school.
Top prize for the life-size
Picasso-ish horse
noble slant to the head
that isn't there.

First rung
of the artist's life.

Who would know
you were thinking of the chair.

Art

        After   *Art Tatum* 13" x 12.5"
                    Gouache and acrylic on mylar.
                    Jennifer Macdonald. 2014

My fleshy face
all moody clouds
ghost swirls
turning into Tatum
the farther you get from me

        bending to the Muse
        to Webster's wails.
        Painted from an album cover
        (Don't play your tune the same way twice.)
        Charcoal? Or the stuff
        that sounds like wash?
        No pores showing.
        Desire.

She's caught me
in the club of smoke
and dreams. Caught me
dreaming dreams
I didn't know I had.

Thief

for Joan

The summer I came back East
friends lent their fine old house

lush window seats, a purple couch.
I felt a spider to the pomegranate.

My friends had lived in Jeddah. Good jewels
and spices. Above one fireplace

his ancestors eyed each other. Hers
did the 18th-century botanicals.

I wanted things
I'd never thought about

sea glass, an idle table.
My friend the poet's library

where I couldn't write.
I fed the birds, the squirrels

myself. At night I quivered over one brown bat.
The day I left went in the poet's kitchen

took the cutting board
carved like a pig.

Salvage

The beams are hemlock. Not the poison bush

the boards that built the Northeast before
they emptied the Pennsylvania woods, Dave says.

The boards are hemlock. Why does this give such pleasure?
I sit on the unfinished stairs to the unfinished basement

a room sprouting up. The studs for the drywall, stroke of luck,
Douglas Fir. The smell of Christmas.

The ceiling was low. Hodgepodge of pipes and cords, electrical.
Cover it up, the first guy said, Do a drop!

Four more bids, the fifth cancels.
I find Dave.

The concrete marbling makes me think of endpaper.
A history of damage. Lino globs, spots of oil.

It's a crappy floor, Dave's sidekick Tony says.
What he used to say about the ceiling. Okay, he'll sand

the floor, wax it down. Dave says, Wait, we'll figure out something better.
Almost Biblical, this willingness to try one thing, another,

why it's taken three months. More. I'm not minding.
Mornings they park their coolers under the old pine table.

We laugh about the Farrelly and Coen brothers. Dave rants
about politics, religion. Tony rants about spending.

He thinks the beams Dave scraped pale are 19th century salvage.
I like this. Salvage to rescue. Salve.

Salvage, a balm. *Salve!*
Welcome.

17

At the good dog park

Dogs handle their differences.
Sniff from the bottom up
know that head to head
things can get ugly. Always

the thrusts for dominance
but in their world
even the alphas take turns.
Rarely an animal's so snarly
she's taken out. Energy's raced off

erased in packs around the turf.
At Schuylkill River Park
always a settling. Snouts
at the trough.

What do I regret?
Not knowing my own thirst.
Not holding my heart's
ground.

Here are the auscultations—
Listen.

When Philip Wu took us to the Chinese banquet

I wore the dress of fine-wale
corduroy plush as the belly
of the spaniel you liked to say
replaced you.

>   You took a Polaroid of Philip and me
>   hugging—inarched. With our black
>   shag caps of hair we were siblings.
>   Happy siblings.

He was your friend first.
Every Thanksgiving he came bearing pleasures:
diamond studs for small Johana, bouquets
for me, Godiva for the table.
When dessert was cleared, he'd hop a chair
pour into *La donna e mobile*.

>   Philip wanted to be known for his singing
>   not the bank. One holiday
>   he brought the big-haired blonde
>   he wanted to marry you called
>   a gold-digger. Next time the girl
>   from Taiwan nearer his age.

He disappeared.
I lost the dress.
I don't remember if it got a rip or a stain
or I gave it to Goodwill.

I miss its touch. The darts
making me glad. Snaps dancing
from the Mandarin collar
to my boots. The skirt was
cut on the bias. It swirled.

>   You left.
>   You said you'd never marry again.
>   You did.

Attend

The daffodils gone crisp
and pulpy where once green.
The sink unfilled.

The toaster on the counter
near the oil, the bread. The peanuts
for the squirrels—

A prayer. The block
of knives, the cutting board,
the pitcher for the wooden

spoons; the one for metal
things. The scrapers, whisks and
water jug. Brush, sponge and

liquid soap.
They wait
on me.

Quodlibet

> *If I can take only one composer to that desert island, it would have to be Bach.*
> Glenn Gould

My friend the poet wants Mozart at his funeral,
the clarinet concerto. I want the Goldberg.
There won't be time for all the variations.
The Aria, aka the Sarabande, should do it
—with repeats.

Unless the Quodlibet?

My friend irks some with his asides:
He'll introduce a music teacher, sing a theme.
I like digression, this puncturing of the wall.

Johana could play the Sarabande herself
but she'll be grieving. Glenn Gould's been chosen
but which version? The first's exuberant tempi?
The last's as joyful, more serene.

If I decide to take my poem somewhere
say Fergie's Pub,
I'll break a wall—

> Who was Herr Goldberg?
> Wherefore the Quodlibet's stolen tunes?
>
> Farty *Kraut und Ruben:*
> Cabbages and turnips have driven you away—if only
> Mother had cooked meat . . .
>
> *Ich bin so lang nicht . . .*
> You have been away so long my love, come closer!

I'm old or maybe grown . . .
The Sarabande's a beauty
but why be solemn? The laughing one
I tell her. No, both!
Come closer.

It is all a matter of hands . . .
    Anne Sexton

Adagio, ma non troppo

>After   Beethoven:
>*String Quartet in E-Flat Major, Opus 127*

Here it comes, that vein of longing from the violin
the voice that is most human. That ache
of presence and of looking back.

Here it comes
that tenderness. And hope.

Somewhere I read he counted sixty beans to make his coffee.
I grind my careless handful and see him walk the outskirts of Vienna
in search of pastorals.

Impossible
to speak of one who lived without the platitudes.

A person should take music lessons
if for no reason than these opportunities for tenderness.

It is all a matter of hands.
Out of the mournful sweetness of touch comes love.

I shouldn't have betrayed you.

Finding Schubert

Dear Schober, I am ill

I have eaten nothing for eleven days and drunk nothing, and I totter feebly from my chair to my bed and back again . . . Be so kind then as to assist me in this desperate situation by means of literature. Of Cooper's I have read the Mohicans, the Spy, the Pilot and the Pioneers. If you have anything else of his I implore you to deposit it with Frau von Bogner at the coffeehouse for me. My brother will most faithfully pass it on to me.
                    Letter to Franz Schober. 11 November. 1828

The songs are on the table. The manuscript,
the medicine, the little library his best friend made for him.

Nineteenth-century Europe couldn't get enough of Fenimore-Cooper.
The bows and arrows of America: escape and politics.

Delirious, he sings. Waking checks the proofs *of Winterreise.*
Slashes notes as if by razor as if the tones were the disease.

Mercury, the cure that kills. Dementia and paralysis, deformities.
Syphilis. The stigma.

Death's not the worst thing that can happen, Schubert tells his brother.

Delirious, he sings. Calls out for Beethoven, for the last quartet.
Into the sickroom they bring their strings.

It's rude to shake a man visible and claim the results.

And still I see him, feverish, enraptured. Marking the score
that scared his friends that cost more effort than any before—

The rimless glasses. Curls curling like the melodies
but no, the illness took them.

> *For some time Schubert appeared very upset and melancholy.*

One day he said, Come over to Schober's and I will sing you a cycle of horrifying songs. So he sang the entire Winterreise through to us in a voice full of emotion. We were utterly dumbfounded by the mournful, gloomy tone of these songs and Schober said that only one, Der Lindenbaum, had appealed to him. To this Schubert replied, I like these songs more than all the rest. Someday you will too.
>
> Joseph von Spaun, Reminiscences, 1858

It's beautiful the manuscript
and messy: his Winter Journey
battered with revisions.

It was my birthday, the first day of spring.
I went to hear the songs that frightened him
that frightened his friends.

The hall was standing room.
A famous baritone sang the Wanderer
who's lost his love.

Love loves to wander, goes the song.
Love turns the weathervane.

Why do you listen to such mournful music?
You said before you left.
Does it matter who betrayed?

Winter can be any season.

Under a lime tree, the Wanderer's
love began. *Der Lindenbaum*, the song.
Ours was non-blooming pear.

It's snowing hard beyond the village
he dreams the hurdy gurdy man.
Old, blind, his fingers numb with cold

Der Leiermann plays
and no one listens.
The Wanderer brings his songs.

The hall was standing room.
Sorrow rippled the hall.

Sonata in B-flat Major

In the living room Walter Klein plays the last sonata.
That unearthly trill—beware the ornament

that isn't ornamental. The left hand warning—
Holding joy.

Repeat. Repeat.
Each time, a deepening.

The major key that sounds like minor
that sounds like pain

or patience.

The summer you returned
that we pretended it wasn't over.

Too late we listen
we learn to listen.

The CD on the shelf
how many years unopened?

On the ceiling in the Spanish Chapel

>After a fresco by Andrea di Bonaiuto
>Santa Maria Novella, Firenze

The ocean tips a boat too small to hold eleven men.
Some stare into the sea. Some stand as I stand, seasick,
looking up at them. Under the swollen mast
one covers his face. Another could be Peter.
The one who makes me want to shout Sit down!

The one who made this fresco understands the dread that sleeps in water.
The worry of the swells. I find his name and learn my apprehension
missed the miracle. Peter kneeling in the sea—
beneath his strolling Lord.

Do you believe in ghosts?
Before the Spanish Eleonora took the space it was the Chapel of the Faults.
Dominicans confessed their sins out loud.
You see them painted on another wall: rows and rows of monks
pretending not to mind. The power of Florence.
The piety.

Sweetgrass:
I can't forget the herding of a hundred thousand sheep
across the Beartooth Mountains. Magnificent, bewildered creatures
caught in blinding white.

The looks upon their faces. The men in Peter's boat.

319 E. 24 St., #25D

for Maria and Walter

God came this morning. Sailed
across the 40-story building stretching
Second Avenue to First: Co-ops
friends call The Lump.
A giant swoosh of white

fat as a porpoise loomed
across their picture window
woke me on the sofa where
I watched the Empire State turn
colors. The Empire State

was gone. The sky at 3:22
was periwinkle. I got the camera phone
the sky was black—
my god dissolved. But

I'd seen the layers. Principalities.
Thrones. I disbelieved, of course.
No choirs disengaged
the ether. Still
I saw wings.

Fermata

       Wait—
Don't throw them out!

She sees me reaching
     for the tulips

Skirts defiant
     spilling gold

The Starlight Room

    for Katrina

He played the Starlight Room.
He sold insurance to the field hands.

He took me through the rows of beans and berries.
See how good we have it?

He took me over causeways of green water
he took me through the groves of cane and oranges.

At the Musicians Local, old people waved
from folding chairs. He talked to everyone.

Where did he take you, sister?

He took me over causeways of green water.
He took me to the fields of strawberries.

We met the week he died.
I say your name and choke

A child again.
It feels like marbles.

He took me through the fields and over causeways.
Where did he take you, sister?

Your mother, the barmaid.
Our father, the piano player.

Looking at your face, my face
with better bones—

I know before he tells me.
He loved both mothers.

Seahorses make good fathers.
One mate forever, eggs in the pouch.

I taste your name:
Oranges for love, papayas for shame.

He took me over causeways of green salty water.
Where did he take you?

Flamboyant

Before I knew its name
I knew that it was royal
the poinciana stretching
past the bedroom window.
It's see-through canopy fluttering
a song without the wind, its slender fingers
more fern than leaf.
A song and not a song.
I was a child
what do we know?

>   I went back home to 29th Street.
>   The house that once slept four of us
>   divided for three families.
>   The tree was gone.

Messy, the woman said.
See the petals littering?
Sparks, I told her.

Notes

"On the ceiling in the Spanish Chapel" refers to a fresco by Andrea di Bonaiuto in the church of Santa Maria Novella in Florence. *Sweetgrass* is the documentary produced by Ilsa Barbash and Lucien Castaing-Taylor filmed in Montana's Absaroka-Beartooth Wilderness.

"Listening to the death of Lorca" refers to *Ainadamar,* Osvaldo Golijov's 2006 opera on the assassination of Federico Garcia Lorca in Granada. *Cante jondo* is an Andalusian folk song. The quotation: *I saw a pomegranate bleeding melodies* belongs to Golijov.

"The pianist speaks" is a meditation on Robert Schumann's song cycles *Dichterliebe* (The Poet Speaks) and *Frauen-liebe und leben* (A Woman's Love and Life). Marlboro is the chamber music festival in Vermont founded by Rudolf Serkin and Adolph Busch..

"Quodlibet," the 30th of the Goldberg Variations, is a canonic juxtaposition of German folk songs. A quodlibet is also a theological argument.

"Adagio, ma non troppo" the expressive instruction for the second movement of the Beethoven Quartet in E-flat Major, Opus 127. The complete heading: Adagio, ma non troppo e molto cantabile: Slow but not too much and very songful. The line *It is all a matter of hands/out of the mournful sweetness of touch comes love* belongs to Anne Sexton.

"Finding Schubert" references the masterpieces composed in the final months of the composer's life: *Winterreise,* a cycle of 24 songs to poems of Wilhelm Mueller, and the final *Sonata in B-Flat Major, D. 960. It's rude to shake a man visual and claim the results"* from Richard Siken's "Portrait of Fryderyk in Shifting Light."

"Flamboyant" is another name for the deciduous Royal Poinciana native to tropical climates. Also a song by the singer Luria.

Gratitude

This book would not be possible without the inestimable rigors of the MFA program of Warren Wilson College. My thanks to faculty mentors Marianne Boruch, Alan Williamson, Daniel Tobin and Gabrielle Calvocoressi, Rodney Jones and Daisy Fried. To Leonard Gontarek for early workshops in Philadelphia, and the New York State Writers Institute for studies with Henri Cole.

I am beyond grateful for the artistry, insight and encouragement of my daughters Jennifer and Johana Macdonald, and for the technical advice of son-in-law Andy P. Swan and brother Sergio Gregory Valdes. For the inspiration of cousin and poet Mary Elizabeth (Betti) Perez, and enormous generosity of friends-become-family Diana and H. James Burgwyn. Where would we be without the kindness of friends: including Paul Boynton, Bonnie Clause, Minna Duchovnay, Trish Marshall, Catherine and David Purnell, Katherine Regan, Ann Zalkind Sullivan, Kathleen Turner, Joyce Thornburg, and Maria and Walter Whitcher. I am indebted to Catherine Grossman for her many and close re-readings of these poems. To Kersti Blumenthal for her keen librarian's eye. Thank you to the Warren Wilson alumni "Wallies," and to the fellowship of the Grind, whose inspiring poets include Daye Phillipo and T. de los Reyes.

Nor would this work be possible without the dedication of my late parents Sergio and Olga Valdes, teachers Nan and R.E. L. Chumbley and Julio Esteban who sustained me at the keyboard. A practice that led to the privilege of covering the incomparable artists, orchestra, and chamber society in the city I most love.

Lesley Valdes grew up in Miami, FL. She comes to poetry following a career in journalism, including posts as classical music critic of *The Philadelphia Inquirer, The San Jose Mercury News* and critic-at-large for the classical and jazz station WRTI, 90.1 FM 90. Her work has appeared in many national publications including *The New York Times, The Wall St. Journal* and *American Poetry Review*. A recipient of awards and fellowships from the National Arts Journalism program of the Pew Charitable Trusts, the Institute for Ramon Llull, Barcelona, and the New York State Institute for Writers and Larry Levis Friends of Writers. Poems have appeared in numerous journals including *Shadowgraph, The Curator, The Boiler, Pantheon, Glint Literary Journal, Schuylkill Valley Review,* and *Women's Voices for Change*. She is a graduate of the Peabody Conservatory of Music, and the MFA program for Writers of Warren Wilson College. She lives in Philadelphia where she is on the faculty of the Fleisher Art Memorial, and an instructor of piano.

www.ingramcontent.com/pod-product-compliance
Lightning Source LLC
Chambersburg PA
CBHW030100170426
43197CB00010B/1602